a smart girl's guide

Drama, Rumors & Secrets

staying true to yourself
in changing times

by Nancy Holyoke
illustrated by Brigette Barrager

Published by American Girl Publishing
Copyright © 2015 American Girl

Questions or comments? Call 1-800-845-0005,
visit **americangirl.com**, or write to Customer Service,
American Girl, 8400 Fairway Place, Middleton, WI 53562-0497.

Printed in China
15 16 17 18 19 20 21 22 LEO 10 9 8 7 6 5 4 3 2 1

Editorial Development: Darcie Johnston
Art Direction and Design: Lisa Wilber
Illustrations: Brigette Barrager
Production: Jeannette Bailey, Judith Lary, Paula Moon, Kristi Tabrizi
Consultant: Jane Annunziata, Psy.D.

Library of Congress Cataloging-in-Publication Data

Holyoke, Nancy.
Drama, rumors & secrets: staying true to yourself in changing times / by
Nancy Holyoke; illustrated by Brigette Barrager.
    pages   cm. — (A smart girl's guide)
ISBN 978-1-60958-903-5 (pbk.) — ISBN 978-1-60958-946-2 (ebook)
1. Girls—United States—Psychology—Juvenile literature. 2. Interpersonal
relations in children—United States—Juvenile literature. 3. Interpersonal
relations in adolescence—United States—Juvenile literature. 4. Social
interaction in children—United States. 5. Social interaction in adolescence—United States. I. Barrager, Brigette, illustrator. II. Title.
HQ777.H637 2015   305.230820973—dc23   2014024148

Dear Reader,

In the following pages, girls like you speak out about drama.

They talk about feuds, gossip, jealousy, competition, teasing, backstabbing, and exclusion—problems that are familiar to almost every girl between the ages of seven and seventeen.

Drama often hits a peak around the time a girl goes to middle school, but it may start a lot earlier. Some girls seem to thrive on it. Others suffer badly. Many feel swept along by a situation that brings out the worst in just about everybody.

As one girl wrote in a post to American Girl: "Drama stinks, but everyone has to deal with it."

This book shows you how to do just that. It explores why drama exists, how a drama starts, what keeps a drama going, and how to cool one down. Along the way, you'll find quizzes that can help you see how friends create drama, and how you might be contributing to it yourself. How can you avoid drama? How can you handle a dramatic friend? What can you do to protect yourself when a drama's raging? That's all here, too.

By the final pages, we hope you have a whole new understanding of what drama is actually about—and a new appreciation for the power you have to stop it.

Your friends at American Girl

contents

feelings rule

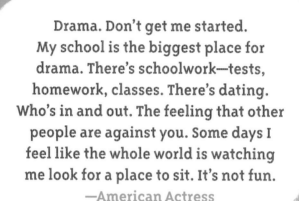

Drama. Don't get me started. My school is the biggest place for drama. There's schoolwork—tests, homework, classes. There's dating. Who's in and out. The feeling that other people are against you. Some days I feel like the whole world is watching me look for a place to sit. It's not fun.

—American Actress

the daily drama

Uh-oh.

Emma's in tears because Gracie and Anna were whispering together on the bus.

Katie sent a mean text to Maya from Liam's phone. Maya yelled at him in the hall.

Ava sat next to Aaliyah again at lunch. Wait till Lila finds out!

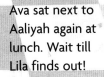

Min-joo is still ignoring Jasmine for spreading rumors about her, even though Jasmine told her that Mikayla bullied her into it.

Three hours after Bianca broke up with Jason, Rachel was talking with him at the bus stop. Now all the soccer girls are saying mean stuff about Rachel online.

Olivia is talking a mile a minute. Is she happy? Is she mad? You don't know. But she's excited, that's for sure.

What's with all the drama?

Everyone's always excited about something. A problem that starts between two people suddenly involves five. Then twenty. One crisis dies down and the next one starts. There are days you'd rather stay in bed with the cat than get up and deal with it all.

People often use the word **drama** to describe making a big deal out of "nothing." But conflicts about little things can really be about big ones, and no drama feels small when you get dragged into it. Drama changes how friends treat friends. It changes how you feel about yourself. The fact is, living with daily drama is a very big deal.

tears and fears

I hate puberty! I've got so many emotions and I can't control them. I feel like my world is falling apart. Help!
—Kidnapped by Puberty

You're not alone! Most people feel torn up by emotions during puberty, and science says there's a very good reason for that.

In puberty, a girl's body produces chemicals called *hormones.* These hormones create physical changes that are easy to see. What you don't see is that those same hormones are also at work on your emotions. The structure of your brain is changing. The way your nervous system works is changing. It's not as obvious as getting taller and curvier, but it's every bit as real.

chemical changes inside the body =
Intense Emotions
and
MOOD SWINGS

Those big, new emotions can get pretty confused by your physical changes. Chances are, you've never been so aware of your body in your entire life—or so worried about how others see you. You compare yourself with your friends. You may compare yourself with models and movie stars. Lots of girls become their own worst critics.

Getting ready in the morning used to take you five minutes. Now your dad has to knock on the bathroom door to get you away from the mirror. You may have days when you walk around all day afraid of the moment someone points a finger at a flaw you're trying to hide. School feels different. You don't want to stick out. You try hard not to make mistakes and to save face when you do.

Along the way, you may start feeling like "you" is just a part you're playing. You're changing so fast. Who can tell who you *are* anymore, anyway?

experiments

Who are you? How do you fit in? Who do you want to be? Now that your body is reinventing itself, you may think it's a great chance to reinvent yourself in other ways, too.

In some ways, it's all a big experiment. Does this shirt seem like you? What music do you want to hear? Do you really want to move up in soccer, or would you rather switch it up and play more tennis? A few years ago, your parents would have made a lot of these decisions. Now they're up to you.

You can also try on some of those strange feelings knocking around inside your chest and see how they fit. What's it like to get mad? What's it like to be romantic? How does it feel to cry? Just what are all these different feelings really about?

Of course, everyone around you is struggling with the same feelings and changes that you are. Friendships are shifting constantly, and you're all keeping track of the results.

Is Chloe getting popular? Is Maddy going Goth? Is Leah sitting with the nerds? And what about you? Do you want to hang out with your new pals from band or the friends you've had since second grade? Do you feel closer to Maria or to Lamae? And does Lamae feel closer to you or to Josie?

School is harder. Activities are intense. And your parents aren't around the way they used to be to protect and guide you.

Put it in a pot and turn the heat on high. What do you get?

DRAMA

Insecurity   PUBERTY   STRESS   COMPETITION   EMOTIONS

friendships

the problem with drama

The drama between Zoey and Trinity has been going three days straight. It's a full-time job keeping up. You finally managed to settle in to work on your presentation, but every time you get an idea, another text pings in.

Drama is crisis. It asks all you can give and then some. You get less sleep at night and less done during the day, and the emotional ups and downs are exhausting. You could be learning to dance, working at a soup kitchen, or biking around the lake. Instead you're caught up in a drama that you can't really do much about and that doesn't directly involve you.

Bottom line: Drama can eat up your life.

Yesterday you told Jaycee your secret. Now she's told it to Taylor. Jaycee is evil. She's ruined your whole life.

When you're in a drama, you're so full of feelings—betrayal, fury, fear, sadness—that the world seems black and white. People and events seem either very, very right or very, very wrong. But in real life not every problem is a catastrophe, and a friend who's made a mistake isn't evil. When you have a problem with a friend, you need to think and plan in order to fix it. Does drama help? Just the opposite.

Bottom line: Drama's a warped view of the world.

One minute you're upset with your friend Ashley. The next you're grounded for yelling at your little sister. Your brother calls you Hurricane Hannah, and in your heart of hearts you *do* feel sort of like a hurricane.

Moods are hard to shake. If you're mad, hurt, and anxious at school, chances are you're going to be mad, hurt, and anxious when you walk in the door at home. Drama with friends can create drama at home, and drama at home can create drama with friends.

Bottom line: Drama makes more drama.

Last month, Sophia decided she didn't like Amber and said you should stop liking Amber, too. Today Sophia said a bunch of bad stuff about Saskia. What if Sophia decides to stop liking Saskia?

When kids create drama, other people get hurt. For some, the hurt is public and agonizing, but no one walks away free. In instances like this, a single girl can poison an entire group by creating an atmosphere of fear, jealousy, and shame. Friends who should be open and free with one another get guarded. There's more plotting and planning. There's less trust. There's less truth. What you share becomes the exact opposite of what we all want from the word "friendship."

Bottom line: Drama hurts people and friendships.

When you're with your friends, you feel fake.

It's natural for a girl to try on different clothes, different ideas, and different ways of expressing herself. There's a little bit of acting mixed up with all that, which is perfectly natural, too. It's about discovering who you are and what kind of person you want to become. The problem is that most girls are nervous about what other people think. Drama expresses those fears. It also makes them bigger. Louder. Girls dealing with daily drama may end up worrying more about how they *appear* than how they truly *are* and what they truly feel. That can make a person feel hollow—and very lonely.

Bottom line: A girl can get lost in drama.

rewrite the script

People may think drama is inevitable. It isn't.
Girls like you can rewrite the script.

Drama's just a bunch of nonsense
about nothing.

This stuff has always gone
on with kids. You can't
stop it.

Girls love drama. They need the
attention. That's just how we are.

I don't need a lot of drama.
I can make different choices.
I can rewrite the script.

I know that other kids are like me.
Everybody wants to fit in some-
where. Everybody's trying hard to
be liked and to figure out what sort
of person she wants to be.

I have strong feelings, just like most
kids. My feelings aren't good or bad.
They just *are*. I feel them. I'm not going
to pretend I don't. But I can control what
I do with them. They don't control me.

I believe in doing what's right.
I'm going to make mistakes.
Everybody does. But I will never stop
trying to be a decent person. I'm
going to grow up liking myself.

among friends

My friends and I fight over some pretty stupid things. It tears us apart for a while, and then we get back together.
—Eva

Drama can be a little fun to watch, I admit. But it is not fun when you are in the drama, because it can break friendships apart.
—No Drama Queen

The drama I see has to do with friends constantly changing friends.
—Julia

Middle school is really harsh. People are all in a hierarchy. It makes being friends hard. Right now, my closest friends are not acting like friends. I have other friends, in different groups, but those groups are higher or lower in the hierarchy, so it would be hard for us to hang out without somebody looking bad. It's all so confusing.
—Sofia

Dramas tend to be based on one thing: exclusion.
—Haley

My friends get in fights a lot. They always make up, but I wish they weren't such drama queens.
—Dana

"sit with us"

You walk into the lunchroom and head straight toward them: your friends. Call them a group, but to you they're more like a family. It's where you belong. They listen when you talk. They care how you feel. You can hang out and be goofy together. You can share secrets. When you're with your friends, you matter. You're special. You're accepted. (They're also what stands between you and being alone in that lunchroom.)

> I have absolutely the most gorgeous, nice, caring friends in the world. I can trust them, and they can trust me.
> —Isabel

> Our friendship is like a triple-knotted shoelace. Not even the strongest person can untie it.
> —Madeline and Gabriella

My friends and I never stay in a fight for long, and eventually we walk off happy. That's how I know we are true friends.
—Abigail

I've found friends who are 100% sincerely nice and who like me for who I am.
—Julia

We're accepting, and we just like to be with each other. We help each other out and don't let rifts get in the way of being friends. We are who we are, and we're fine with that.
—MT

us and them

All groups have a way of thinking about themselves. It comes partly from the kids in the group—what they share, how they see themselves, and how they'd like to be seen. It comes partly from how kids outside the group see it. Usually there are lots of labels floating around, like "geeks," "brainiacs," "jocks," and of course, "popular."

However that works, everybody has a pretty good sense of where everybody fits, and friends often find ways to celebrate their friendship—and show their loyalty.

It's natural to like the things your friends like. If everybody in your group wears daisy clogs, you may decide to start wearing daisy clogs, too. If your friends have pierced ears, you may want to pierce yours, too. That's OK, so long as you really want to wear daisy clogs and have your ears pierced.

But what if you don't?

What if all your friends wear black and you show up in plaid? If you stop listening to country and start liking indie? If you start spending time with a girl outside your group?

e wear jeans

e wear leggings
nd LOTS of pink!

LOVE TO LISTEN TO MUSIC

We have boyfriends

: like to read and get good grades.

VE LIKE THE NERDS BUT
HINK THE POPULAR
KIDS ARE STUCK-UP.

We don't want
boyfriends yet!

Some groups are relaxed. Being friends doesn't involve a lot of dos and don'ts. Friends don't spend time examining what other friends wear or do or say. They don't question one another's loyalty. They also aren't hung up on disliking kids in other groups or excluding people. Girls have friends in and outside the group, and that's fine. Kids do pretty much what they like to do.

But other groups are strict. People are really critical. Friends tell friends how to dress and what to think, who's OK to talk to and who isn't. There's always a right way and a wrong way, and the group decides which is which. People ridicule kids outside the group, and nobody feels safe inside. A girl feels she's one mistake away from getting kicked out.

Sometimes a girl falls in with a group without knowing what she's signed on for.

23

membership dues

Which answer best describes how things work in your group of friends?

1. Gabby says, "That band is so lame," and the other girls agree. You say, "I love that band." The others . . .

   a. ask what you like about it.   **b.** laugh and say you have no taste.

2. You and Sarah have been having a blast in science, so you invite her to sit with you and your friends at lunch. Your friends . . .

   a. talk and laugh with you and Sarah, just like normal.   **b.** act like a cat left a dead mouse at their door.

3. Layla and Jessica got in a fight over Gavin, and your friends all think it was Layla's fault. It goes without saying that . . .

    a. how you behave with Layla is your own business.   **b.** you'll ignore Layla in the hall.

4. Destiny tells Camilla, "If you don't come to the show, you're not our friend anymore." The others say . . .

    a. "Come off it, Destiny."   **b.** "And we want the friendship bracelet back, too!"

5. When your friends look out across the lunchroom, they see . . .

    a. other kids.   **b.** snobs, losers, dorks, and jerks.

Answers

The rules for these two types of groups are pretty clear:

"a" rules	"b" rules
We have our own opinions.	We think alike.
Our motto is: Welcome.	Our motto is: Keep out!
Threats are not cool.	Break a rule, you get punished.
We're like everyone else.	We're better than everyone else.
Difference is fine.	If you're different, we laugh.

If you checked **all a's,** your group doesn't have membership dues. Friendship is freely given because you all like one another. Each girl feels like she can be herself.

If you checked **mostly b's,** a girl gives a lot to belong to your group. Your days are shaped by your friends' expectations. You can't express yourself without getting criticized. You can't make new friends freely. Worse, you're learning to treat kids outside the group as if they're worth less than you are. It's a high price to pay for friendships that don't make you feel good.

bffs

Of course, not all friends are created equal. In a larger group of friends, some girls are closer than others. That may create some tension.

At my school there is a lot of drama about who is whose best friend.
—Ella

My two besties don't like each other. They are fighting over me like two dogs over a bone.
—Frustrated Friend

I have two best friends. They like me, but they tell each other secrets they don't tell me.
—Lydia

My best friend is avoiding me. I'm getting clingy. I know she doesn't like it, but I'm afraid of being dumped.
—Desperate

In the past few years, I've been really mean to this one girl. She's my BFF's friend. I'm jealous and I get angry a lot.
—D.B.

My best friend is in a different homeroom. Now she'll be BFFs with somebody else.
—HMS

None of this is easy. But there are some big truths underlying these close friendships. Whether you're enjoying a new friend or missing an old one, it helps to keep them in mind.

The Basics on BFFs

1. Friendship can only be given. You can't demand it. You can't argue your way into it. You can't tell another girl how to feel—and she won't like it if you try.

2. Friends need freedom. If you are too possessive—if you hold on to a friend too hard—sooner or later she'll resent it. Part of being a good friend is allowing your "bestie" to have fun with other people, too.

3. Friends aren't for ranking. You'll be happier if you think of your friends as a circle of people—not a list of your preferences, where everybody's ranked 1, 2, 3, and on down the line. Being less exclusive gives you more friends. It gives you healthier friendships. And when the day comes that you lose an important friend, you'll have others to turn to.

4. Calling somebody your BFF doesn't make it true. Deep friendships grow out of honesty and trust. You can't get a good friend—or be one—just by trading necklaces.

5. Relationships are always changing. As you get older, some friends will drift away. Others will stay with you, as new friends appear and get folded into the mix. It's all a part of growing up.

6. A great friendship never dies completely. When friends treat each other kindly, their relationship may go to sleep for a while, only to wake up again years later. For instance, you may hardly notice your best friend from third grade when you walk down the halls now, but you two might cross paths unexpectedly in high school and hit it off all over again. Friends that endure over time can become the best of besties and last the rest of your life.

behind the scenes

When there's drama, girls may take on various parts backstage in the production—and some of them aren't helpful. Could any of these describe you?

1.
When there's drama, you go to work. You talk to everybody. Then you talk to everybody again. And again. Everyone's excited, and you're in the middle of it.

2.
Your best friend is super, super popular. She runs the show, and you get to help. Whatever she wants— you'll make it happen.

3.
You want to fit in with your friends. You wear what they wear, do what they do, say what they say. Sometimes following along makes you feel bad, but you hide it.

4.

You know everybody's secrets, and you like that. Whenever you want, you let a secret drop and put another kid in the spotlight.

5.

You look great, you act nice, and kids compete to be your friend. Friends pretty much do whatever you say. If they don't—well, bad things happen.

6.

Your friends make fun of you. They exclude you. They embarrass you. You do nothing because you have no choice. If you complained, they'd kick you out of the group.

Answers

What's going on behind the scenes with you?

If you chose 1, you're in publicity. When a drama's brewing, you spread the news, sell the tickets, and pack the house. Stirring up all this interest makes you feel important, but it also makes small problems big, and others suffer for that.

If you chose 2, you're the director's assistant. That gives you power you wouldn't have otherwise. But being a gofer is pretty much about taking orders. And if your whole identity is tied up with this one relationship, that isolates you from everyone else.

If you chose 3, you're into costumes. You know how to keep your head down, blend in, and keep up a good appearance. This protects you from a lot of bad drama, but it doesn't help you form rich relationships or feel good inside.

If you chose 4, you're running lights. You may feel powerful, throwing attention here and there on other kids. But the day will come when kids notice you up there in the darkness. That's the day they'll go from trusting you a lot to not trusting you at all.

If you chose 5, you're being the director. You run the show, which is what you want, in theory. But staying on top is hard work. Power you have. True friends? Not so much. Truth to tell, your days are lonely and not all that much fun.

If you chose 6, you've decided there's nothing you can do to change your situation. It's not true. A girl can decide for herself what parts she cares to play with her friends—and what parts she doesn't. You can make different choices. It's time to step outside the cage you've got yourself in and make them.

Step outside.

There are plenty of parts to play in a group that allow you to express who you really are. Here are a few of them.

The free agent

She has good friends in the group, but she's got friends in other groups, too. That gives her confidence. People see that she's not bound to anybody's rules but her own—and they respect that.

The voice of reason

She's calm. When emotions run high, other girls come to her. She helps them cool down, focus, and fix problems. She doesn't tell anybody what to think or how to feel. She makes suggestions, but she doesn't position herself between the people who are having trouble. Her motto is, "Don't make it bigger."

The plain speaker

She says what she thinks. She doesn't make a big deal out of it. She just doesn't cook her words to please other people. It's a daily thing—a habit. Because she gets so much practice, she's good at it. When a tough situation comes along, she can handle it the way she does the easy ones: honestly.

scenes from a drama

Zombies

It's been a month since the field trip, but your friends are still analyzing every move Kara and Seth made that day. There is absolutely nothing new to say—nada, zip—but everyone keeps talking about it anyway. You're like zombies! *Must talk about Kara and Seth, must talk about Kara and Seth . . .*

Some dramas refuse to die. When you and your friends are stuck in one, you may feel like it's eating away at your brain tissue. It's the same old stuff, over and over again—none of it solving anything and all of it going nowhere. It's beyond boring. What to do? Open your mouth and say: "OK, guys, let's change the subject."

Good drama

Molly posted something ugly about your friend Shawna. You go up to Molly in the lunch line and say, "What you said about Shawna isn't true. You should take it down and apologize to her." Never, ever was the lunchroom so quiet. For once, Molly doesn't have a comeback. By the time you get back to your seat, the news is all over the school.

Some dramas are good, and this is one of them. You stood up for a friend against a powerful girl. It was brave. Kids are talking about you because they know that. You did the right thing, and that sent a bolt of joy through every kid who's been intimidated by someone like Molly. If people are talking about this next week (which they will be), that's great. The best stories have heroes, and in this

story the hero is you.

Switcheroo

Caitlin has always been your best friend. She still is, sort of—only not when she's with her other friends. If she's with them, she does a big switcheroo and pretends you don't exist.

It's hard to know what's going on with a friend like this. She may be temporarily caught up in some unhappy role with these other girls. She may be exploring new friendships, experimenting with a new sense of who she is or might want to be. But this much is clear: She's treating you poorly. So find a private moment and tell her how you feel and how you'd like things to change ("I feel hurt when you don't even say hi in the halls. If we're friends, we should be able to talk, no matter what groups we're in.") How she responds will tell you whether she wants to keep the friendship alive or not. Either way, now's a good time for you to grow other friendships. Caitlin is changing, and you'll need to change, too.

Not a game

Mary Beth is in a fight with Louisa. Every day you pump her for the latest and tell her what to do. Then she does it. It's like one of those games that require a lot of strategy. There are so many people involved by now, it's super complicated and (to be honest) super fun.

Giving advice can be an act of friendship. Entertaining yourself with a friend's dilemma is not. Mary Beth is a person, not a game piece. She needs to solve her own problems, and you need to step back from the drama and let her do it.

are you a drama queen?

Could this be you? Answer yes or no.

1. Bailey walks in with a new purse. "What are you doing with my grandma's purse?" you say. Everybody laughs. You keep going all night with the purse jokes. You love making your friends laugh. Maybe you'll be on TV when you grow up.

yes   no

2. What a day! You've been texting nonstop. First Silas dropped Abby. Then Fernanda was flirting with Joel. The war between Alli and Shetara exploded online, AND something totally embarrassing happened to Jing, which you'd be telling Missy about right now, but the battery on your phone died.

yes   no

3. Nothing's going on, so you tell Skylar that Pedro really likes her. "You should go over and talk to him," you say. She does, and you and your other friends crack up at what happens next.

HA HA HA HA HA HA HA

yes   no

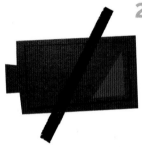

4. Shoshana says she likes Luke, even though you already told everybody Luke and Nyajah would look cute together. Talk about annoying. You start a rumor about Shoshana.

yes   no

5. Last week you and Aubrie got in a fight. She apologized, but you are still talking about how hurt you were. "Maybe you should just let it go," a friend suggests wearily. What?! Let it go?!?! You are soooooooooo hurt that she would say that!

yes   no

6. You text Paige: "Maria's being super friendly to Oscar!" Paige has a huge crush on Oscar. So do you, and any moment now—when Maria's phone rings and Paige starts yelling at her—the person talking with Oscar will be you.

yes   no

Answers

The more yes's you checked, the more you love drama. You love being center stage, having an audience, and expressing yourself. You don't react small—you react BIG. You like to make things exciting. You like a world full of exclamation points!!!!!!!!!! It's more fun! Boo on boredom!!!!

But stop for a moment and think about how this looks from where your friends sit. You'll make fun of a friend if it lets you shine. You'll make others uncomfortable to entertain yourself. You want a lot of attention. Worse, you may get so comfortable creating dramas that you cook up trouble between other people simply to get something you want. While you're lost in the excitement of the moment, your friends are likely feeling hurt, annoyed, overwhelmed, and just plain exhausted.

Don't let your own dramatics get between you and your friends. Dial it down. Go ahead and try out for the school play, but keep your friendships genuine. Your friends will like you more. And when your head hits the pillow at the end of the day, you'll like yourself more, too.

rewrite the script

People may think drama is inevitable. It isn't.
Girls like you can rewrite the script.

To be happy, you have to
get into a good clique.

I can't go against
my group.

If I get friendly with
the wrong people, my friends
will dump me.

I want to get popular.
If I get a chance to move up,
I have to take it.

I can be friends with anyone
I want to be friends with.

Being friends doesn't mean being the
same—or thinking the same. I'm not
going to criticize my friends for being
different, and I'm going to expect
them to accept me in the same way.

My friends aren't rungs on a ladder. I'm
going to make friends with the people
who make my heart sing—not the people
who will make me more popular.

Friendship shouldn't be a power
struggle. I'm not going to set
rules for my friends to follow,
and if they try it on me, I'll ask
them to stop.

I love my friends, and I
care what they think. But
they don't decide what
I do. I'm responsible for
my own choices.

angry & annoyed

When my friend gets mad, she won't talk to me and keeps on giving me the stinkeye. Then the next day she acts all nice, like nothing happened.
—Erin

The drama I face happens when my friends and I don't choose our words carefully. Sometimes we say mean things that we don't really mean.
—Amanda

39

what do you do when you're mad?

Which sounds most like you?

1. Ever since Emma started liking Samuel, you've felt second best. You . . .

   a. tell Emma, "You're getting so stuck-up."

   b. tell Emma you feel sad and ignored, and would like to spend more time with her.

   c. say nothing—and get madder every day.

   d. invite five other girls over on Saturday and leave Emma out.

2. Moira told Jin-soo that you like Gabe. Argh! You . . .

   a. tell Moira she's an awful person.

   b. tell Moira you're upset and you expect her to keep your secrets better in the future.

   c. ignore it. If you got mad, Moira would just get mad back.

   d. tell every kid in science that Moira likes Evan.

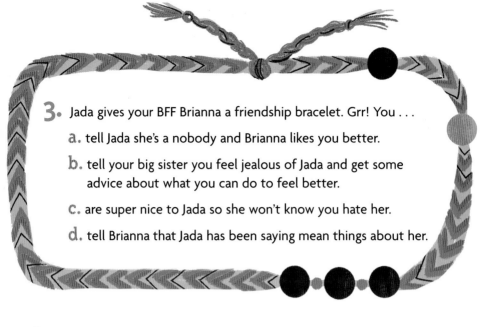

3. Jada gives your BFF Brianna a friendship bracelet. Grr! You . . .

   a. tell Jada she's a nobody and Brianna likes you better.

   b. tell your big sister you feel jealous of Jada and get some advice about what you can do to feel better.

   c. are super nice to Jada so she won't know you hate her.

   d. tell Brianna that Jada has been saying mean things about her.

4. Yesterday, your little sister sang her donkey song for you and Rose. Now Rose is making fun of her. You . . .

   a. call Rose a name and tell her to shut up.

   b. say, "My sister loves that song. Don't make fun of her. It's mean, and it hurts my feelings."

   c. do nothing. If you pretend it's not happening, maybe Rose will stop.

   d. tell everyone how Rose bombed the Spanish test.

5. You lent your favorite sweater to Dominique. You've asked for it back three times. Today she walks in and says, "Oopsie. Sorry. Forgot!" You . . .

   a. say, "So, are you just stealing my sweater or what?"

   b. say, "I've asked you to give my sweater back three times. It's upsetting. I really want it back. I'm going to stop by your house after school and pick it up."

   c. say, "No problem." It wouldn't be nice to get mad.

   d. give her the silent treatment all day. When she asks what's wrong, you say, "Nothing."

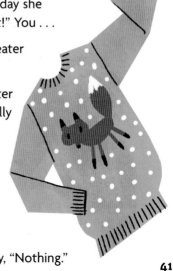

Answers

What *do* you do when you're mad?

If you checked **mostly a's,** you blow.
When you're mad or hurt, you lash out. Your friends get punished before they have a chance to change course or apologize. Sometimes they may not even be sure why you're mad. You never actually stop and tell them what the problem is. Next time, try hitting "pause" before you react. Look for words that explain instead of words that wound. That's what will help make a bad situation better.

If you checked **mostly b's,** you try to fix the problem.
When you're mad or hurt, you say so, and you find a good way to say it, too. Your friends know why you're upset with them, and what you want them to do next. All this keeps the air clear, cuts down the drama, and leaves you feeling lighter for having said what you think.

If you checked **mostly c's,** you absorb the hurt.
You think that getting mad is bad—that if you admit to being upset, you're not being "nice." It's just not true. A girl can express hurt and anger in ways her friends can respond to and respect. If you don't learn to do that, your anger is going to burn you up inside. You'll like yourself less, and your problems will be going nowhere.

If you checked **mostly d's,** you attack
(but pretend you're not doing it).
If you're mad at a girl, you may exclude her, embarrass her, undermine her friendships, or hurt her reputation. Or you may just mess with her mind by freezing her out. The one thing you *don't* do is admit you're mad. You hurt your friends, lose their trust, and gain nothing. You don't even get to say what you're really feeling.

being in a fight

A lot of girls have trouble saying "I'm mad" or "I'm hurt."
Instead they send out the message in a hundred other ways.

rolling eyes

weird eyebrow

exchanging glances

Secret smile

silence

whispering

Whoa! This girl is NOT feeling friendly.
What's up? What's the problem?

Why are you so mad?

Mad? Who, me?

Yes, you!

43

You know how it works:

A girl can send hostile signals with how she stands, looks, and sits.

She can leave a friend out and pretend she didn't mean to.

She can stir up trouble with gossip and rumors.

She can make fun of a friend . . .

> Just kidding!

and deny that it's hurtful.

> Can't you take a joke?

She can make a friend question her own feelings . . .

> You're so sensitive.

and her own judgment.

> No, I didn't. You just imagined it.

When a girl denies what she's doing, it can drive a friend crazy.

> Am I being too sensitive?

> Am I imagining it?

> This feels all wrong, but maybe it's my fault!

> Did that just happen?

> If I apologize, will this stop?

So why do girls express anger this indirect way?

It's easier—and safer.

A girl doesn't have to explain what her problem is.

She doesn't have to have a big, scary discussion, which she might lose.

She can get other girls to side with her, because they hear only her version of things.

Other people won't think she's mean, because she can always deny what she's doing.

Is this the best way to solve a problem?

No! It doesn't solve the problem at all. Freezing out a friend tells her that you're mad. It can make her suffer. It can make her surrender. But what it does NOT do is acknowledge the situation that made one girl so mad to begin with. To do that, you need to communicate openly. You need to talk.

friendship fix-up

Something happened. Now you're unhappy with a friend.
What do you do?

Name your feelings.

You're upset. What exactly are your feelings about?
Are you mad? Sad? Hurt? Scared? Ashamed? Stop and
figure out exactly what's going on inside you and why
you're feeling that way.

Get the words right.

Get everything that's happened clear in your head.
Write it down, if that helps. Be specific. What did
you see and hear? How did you feel? Avoid words
that accuse and words like "always" and "never."
Push yourself to stick with the facts.

~~Desiree's backstabbing me and being mean.~~
↘ I should be specific

Desiree and Lauren were whispering about
me on the bus.

Desiree ignored me in the hall after music.

Ava told me that Desiree told her I'm
stuck-up.   be MORE specific ↘

Desiree and Lauren were whispering on the
bus. I think it was about me, because they
were looking at me. I felt hurt and scared,
wondering what they were saying.

Desiree walked past me without talking in
the hall after music. I felt hurt.

Ava said, "Desiree says you've been
bragging about soccer."

Practice.

You'll have to talk to this girl. Is that scary? Maybe. But it's the only way to set things right. So look into a mirror and practice using your "right words." Practicing will make you better at saying what you have to say and give you confidence.

Explain.

Find a private time to approach your friend, when you can talk face-to-face. (This is definitely not a time to talk online.) Tell her what you think has happened and how you feel about it. Be sure she knows you're interested in solving the problem, not in attacking her.

Hear your friend out.

Ask her what she thinks. Then listen. And don't correct her—no matter how much you want to. She has to have her say, too. Remember that your friend hasn't been practicing, like you have, so it may take a while for her to find her own "right words."

Be patient.

Give yourselves some time, and see if you can find things to agree on.

You: When you're with Lauren, I feel like you're against me.

Desiree: We're not against you. Honest.

You: Lauren is cool, but I don't feel as close to her as I do to you.

Desiree: I know. I wish we had more classes together.

Desiree: I'm sorry we were talking about you.

You: I'm sorry I got jealous.

Desiree: You really *did* win the last soccer game for us.

47

escaping the drama

A drama can suck up every kid within miles. What do you do when you feel yourself getting pulled in? Here are some simple things that help a lot.

Do things you love.

What do you love to do? It could be water ballet, soccer, tae kwon do, theater, drawing, science club, dancing, writing, singing, kayaking, skateboarding, or tennis. Whatever it is, if it makes you happy, now's the time to get out there and *do* it. Connect with new people. Be creative. Run hard and feel your heart beat. If you don't have a big passion, that's OK. You can still sign up for a team, take classes in something fun, or join a club. It will keep your brain and body active, lighten your mood, and give you skills you can be proud of.

Have some friends outside of school.

Chances are, you know some nice girls outside of school. Stop and think who they are: That girl in choir? Your old friend who ended up at a different school? Ariana from gymnastics? Your cousin Julie Mae? Try to build up some of these friendships. For one thing, it'll be fun. For another, it gives you a friend or two who's not part of the daily drama. That's fresh air and blue skies on days when other friends are upset.

Help others.

Step outside the door and volunteer. Tutor younger kids in math. Read to the elderly in a nursing home. Sort clothes with your mom at the local thrift shop. Take care of abandoned animals at a local shelter. Guaranteed: Your world will get bigger, and your own problems will seem smaller.

Find a "favorite aunt."

There are times it's nice to have an older girl to talk to. It could be a sister, an actual aunt, a cousin, or a high-school girl from down the block. Look around for someone you like and trust—a person you can go to for advice. She will have been through what you're going through now and come out the other side. Think of her as your future self! You'll be that wiser, older girl yourself soon.

Today isn't forever.

When things are bad, today feels like forever—that's for sure. But today is *not* forever. It's not, it's not, it's not. Things change over time. Keep telling yourself that. Time helps.

scenes from a drama

A big deal

Paula calls you every day for help in math. She doesn't even bother to read the book! She expects you to do it for her! You don't want to make a big deal of this, so you help her, but you also start making fun of her at lunch.

Anger isn't like water. You can't bottle it up and expect it to stay there. Anger wants to come out. If you don't express it directly, you'll express it indirectly—whether you plan on doing it or not. So say the true thing: "Paula, we're friends, and friends help each other. But I feel like you're always asking me for answers that are right there in the book. I can help you, but I can't do your work for you." Paula may be upset at first, but if you express yourself kindly, chances are she'll change, and your friendship will be better for it. As it is, you're overworked. You're mad inside. You're doing things that hurt your friend—and she has no clue why. Isn't that a big deal, too?

Saving face?

Clara has tears in her eyes. She's so mad she's shaking. You know you're in the wrong, but if you admit what you did, everybody will hate you. You have to fight back!

It's scary. OK . . . it's *really* scary to be face-to-face with someone you know has good reason to be mad at you. But what you really have to do is admit your mistake. It's what being a decent person is all about. If you try to save face, the whole mess will just keep going, and you'll still be trying to save face three months from now. Put a stop to it now! Be brave. Say what you did and say you're sorry.

Eating gravel

Olivia didn't always make fun of you. She used to be nice. Once in a while she still is, and you get up every morning hoping that today will be one of the good days. She's a really cool person, and she *is* your best friend.

You remember what it was like when Olivia was kind. You know how that felt, and you know how you feel now—miserable. You're telling yourself this is OK when you know it's not. This girl is feeding you a steady diet of gravel. It's weighing you down, making you less sure of yourself every day. The biggest danger isn't that Olivia will drop you if you demand to be treated kindly (which, by the way, you should!). The biggest danger is that you'll get used to accepting this behavior as friendship.

War!

You are *so* mad at Amy! You tell Breanna what she's done. You and Cybil don't say a single word to her on the field trip. You tell her secrets to Daniella, and you start a rumor with Evan. Then you post some anonymous comments about Amy online. This is war!

Hold on a minute. You're mad. Understood. You may have very good reasons to be. But that doesn't mean you're free to attack this girl. It doesn't mean you've got the right to be mean, violate confidences, or hurt her reputation. Anger is a feeling—not a reason for bad behavior. You need to talk to Amy directly, tell her how you feel, and explain what you want her to do to make things right. That gives you a chance to express yourself and her a chance to respond. And it's a whole lot healthier than nursing your anger in secret while stirring up trouble behind her back.

rewrite the script

People may think drama is inevitable. It isn't.
Girls like you can rewrite the script.

Nice girls don't
get mad.

It's safer to lie than to say
what I feel.

If I say I'm upset, my friends'
feelings will get hurt.
Or they'll dump me.
Or attack me.

I'm scared of
being mad!

Everybody gets mad sometimes. Feeling mad doesn't make me a bad person. It doesn't make my friends bad, either.

All people disagree sometimes. Disagreeing can help solve problems that would get bigger if they're ignored.

I can disagree with my friends in a way that respects both them and me.

When I'm mad or hurt, I'm going to say so. I'm not going to deny it and then go do something hurtful behind the other person's back.

I can admit when I'm wrong. It's scary, but I'll do it.

When two people have a problem, they have to solve it face-to-face—not working through other kids. I am strong enough to do that.

rumors, secrets & cyberspace

People say things online that they won't say in person.
—AG Fan

People think technology is a game, and you can do and say anything you want. But what you say online can hurt people just as much as if you said it to their face.
—Sarah

If friends would just try to communicate better and not gossip, a lot of drama wouldn't happen.
—An AG Reader

At my school, the main drama is gossip. Everybody gossips about someone different and spreads rumors about that person. One time I was the victim, and it really hurt me inside. When I saw people whispering about me, I went up to them and said, "Guys, this is not cool."
—Katie

My best friend always tells me secrets about other people. I feel bad about it, because these other people don't know what she's doing. I have to wonder whether I can trust her with MY secrets. She's my best friend, but who knows who she's telling.
—Anonymous

Girls start rumors, hear rumors, and spread rumors every day. A lot of times we don't even realize we're saying something mean— we're just talking. But rumors can make people's lives miserable and leave marks forever.
—C. in MI

talk vs. gossip

Friends talk about friends all the time. Kids talk about other kids.

It's natural. You and your friends talk about what you care about, and that includes other people. All this talking connects you. It's a big part of being friends.

What's the difference between that natural sharing and gossiping? It's not always easy to say. What one person takes as gossip, another person may defend as good communication.

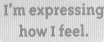

So how are you to judge what you can say freely and what you shouldn't?

Before you start talking—or send that text or post the comment—ask yourself these questions:

Are you talking about something another person considers private?

Would you totally change what you're saying if the person you're talking about appeared?

If this person found out what you're saying, would she feel mad or hurt? And would you feel guilty?

Are you making another kid look bad? Are you hurting his reputation? Are you damaging her friendships?

Are you saying things to make yourself more powerful or popular? Or to make someone like you?

Is this just feeding a drama?

If any answer is **yes,** it's a red flag. You're over the line. Call it "talking" or call it "gossiping"—it's hurtful.

> Honestly? I gossip. Everybody gossips. But I guess it's more fun to gossip about other people than to have people gossip about you.
> —Lily

Precisely. And that's why you should let your answers to these questions help you decide what to say—and what not to.

words on a screen

Texts, e-mail, photo messaging, web pages, blogs, chat rooms, discussion groups, online gaming— the ways kids communicate increase every day, and that's great. Technology lets you make plans with your friends, work together on projects, post schedules, send nice messages at important (and unimportant!) moments, and share a hundred things you love to share, from photos to music to a good laugh over the latest cat video. (Goat videos are pretty great, too.)

That said, talking online is very different from talking face-to-face, and those differences let gossip and drama flourish.

No faces, no clues

When you're talking face-to-face, you have all sorts of clues about what the other person is thinking. You can read a friend's feelings in her face, in her body, in her voice. She may nod her head if she agrees with what you're saying. If she's bored, her eyes may drift off to something behind you. If she's annoyed, you'll see that, too. You may change what you're saying (and how you're saying it) depending on what you see. And, of course, your friend is "reading" you at the same time. Even on the phone, you can get clues from the other person's voice.

But when words are going back and forth on a screen? It's a whole different deal. A smiley may help signal a mood, but there is far less to go on.

No brakes, no sympathy

Writing, you're inside your own head. *Tap, tap, tap.* Send! *Tap, tap, tap.* Send! You're in the zone—juggling words. You aren't thinking about the consequences the way you do when you're looking at a face. It's easy to get carried away. You may say too much and regret it. You may say what you mean poorly and be misunderstood. You may also get harsher—more sarcastic. It's "only a text," so you may say things you'd be too nice to say in person and may not even really believe.

No consequences

Things get ten times worse when people write anonymously. Writing anonymously gives a person the exciting sense that she can try on a whole new personality. A girl may let her emotions run without check. She no longer needs to be nice. She can say and do all kinds of things without answering for it, and she can pretend it doesn't have consequences in the real world, when of course it has big ones.

> No one thinks you're funny.

No privacy, no escape

People share, people forward, people post. Conversations go public, and problems between kids play out in front of the whole world. Kids end up on display at the worst possible moment, with nowhere to hide. If somebody wants to hurt or humiliate somebody else, it's hard to imagine a better tool for the job than a phone, tablet, or computer. And sadly, when friends fight, or people break up, or someone is jealous or wants revenge, that's where kids often turn: to their devices.

No kidding

Devices are fun and helpful, but if people lose control of how they use them, others get hurt.

you and your devices

Who's running the show—you or your devices?

1. Ping! It's the 12th text from Zoe. You are both super upset. You . . .

    a. walk the dog while you cool down. Then you call Zoe and talk it out.

    b. write back instantly—what else? And you do the same thing every five minutes for the next three hours.

2. You write something very, very personal to Livia, which you would die if anyone else saw. For a brief moment, you remember that you don't trust Livia. You . . .

    a. trash the message.

    b. send the message. It felt so good to write. Why waste it?

3. You're on chat with Melany. She's rubbing you the wrong way, and a red light comes on in your brain. *Temper! Temper!* You say . . .

    a. "I'm tired, Melany. I'm signing off. Let's talk about this tomorrow before school."

    b. "WHAT'S YOUR PROBLEM? CAN YOU JUST LET IT GO FOR ONCE?"

4. Gabriel posts a super-awkward picture of you with the caption: "LOL. Just what ARE you doing here, Ellie?" You . . .

a. ignore it.

b. immediately write a long explanation about sticky rice noodles.

5. You're texting with Hailey. Bradon sits down and says, "Say hi from me." You say . . .

a. "Hi from Bradon."

b. "Bradon just landed from Planet Dork. I think he's sweet on u!! Don't u ♥ his cute eyebrows? ;)"

Answers

If you answered **mostly a's,** you have a healthy relationship with your devices. You know when they're helpful and when they're not. You're focused on real people, real situations, and what you really think—not on messaging.

If you answered **mostly b's,** you're operating on autopilot. You respond before you think. You message when you're anxious. You message when you're mad. All this makes you less pleasant. It also makes you more vulnerable. You're oversharing, even when it may cause you grief. You're taking the bait when people tease you, even when doing so opens you up for more.

It's a common thing: People get so used to getting and sending messages, they don't feel normal without a phone in their hands. But sending and receiving 24/7 is *not* normal. It's only a habit. You can break it, and you'll have better relationships if you do. You should own your device. Don't let it own you.

rumors

Rumors don't come out of nowhere.
People create them—and the recipe is *not* appetizing.

Recipe for a Rumor

(Feeds one school for weeks)

Step 1: Select your ingredients. Find a topic (and a target). A lot of rumors start out as a problem between two people. So think: Are you in a fight with a friend? Jealous of someone? A rumor can offer revenge. You can trash the kid online. You can wreck the reputation of one person to impress somebody else. Just think up a story!

Step 2: Add gossip and stir. You want this rumor to grow. So spread the word. Send texts. Post some posts. Are there two sides to a story? Ignore them. Are important details left out? Who cares! Exaggerate the juicy parts. Don't worry about being fair or accurate. This *is* a rumor, after all.

Step 3: Season with emotions. Be outraged! Be shocked! Laugh at others' mistakes! React BIG! It makes the rumor seem exciting and important, even if it's small and silly.

Step 4: Beat the topic daily. Don't let it rest. A rumor never has a single cook. Repeat a rumor, and you're in the kitchen along with whoever started it.

Step 5: Cook online. If you post a bunch of nonsense after dinner, in the morning half the school may think it's true. That's the weird magic of the printed word: People tend to believe it. People also tend to go with the crowd. An entire school may consider something common knowledge when there isn't an ounce of truth in it.

> That sounds AWFUL.

Awful, indeed.

But let's be honest: Rumors exist because they entertain people. A scandal can liven up a boring day. A person can also feel a bit better about herself when someone *else* has made a mistake. (She probably feels safer, too, when the spotlight is trained on another girl.)

Of course, if the rumor is about you, it's incredibly hurtful and often incredibly unfair. So here's what a girl *really* should do as far as rumors go:

Be skeptical of the facts.

Don't believe everything you hear. How does the person telling you a story know what she supposedly "knows"? Was she there when this thing happened, or is she just repeating something she's heard? Why is she telling you this, anyway? What does she get out of the situation?

Be skeptical of yourself, too.

We all tend to believe what we want to believe. We also tend to believe what we fear might be true. It's human nature. Before you jump on the bandwagon, ask yourself what makes you want to help this rumor along.

And if the story is true, so what?

Say someone has made a mistake. Someone has embarrassed herself horribly. The story is true. Do you really want to be one more person who won't let her forget it? Treat this girl the way you'll want others to treat you the day you make your own embarrassing mistake.

Don't be afraid to speak up.

"That's just a rumor. I don't buy it." "Why should I believe that?" "Why are we talking about this?" "Who says?" Ask a few simple questions, and a big, important rumor can go *poof* and vanish before your very eyes.

63

rules of the road

There are some common rules for people online and with phones.
Do you know them? Let's find out. What's a good move? What's not?
Answer thumbs-up or thumbs-down.

1. When you write something to a friend, you consider how much you trust her and how you would feel if the message went public.

2. You don't share your passwords—except with your closest friends.

3. Jacie's message makes you laugh so hard you spill soda all over creation. If you forward it, Ethan will laugh, and Sara will ♥ you for sharing. But Jacie might want to keep it private, so you do.

4. Anjali's upside down. Her mouth's open, her hair is a mess, and her eyes are goofy. You click. Funniest photo *EVER*. While Anjali yells "no!" you send it to Ciara. Ciara won't share it. And anyway, Anjali's done stuff like this to you.

5. Your BFF asks, "So, what are you doing right now?" The answer is that you're sitting on your bed in your nightie experimenting with a curling iron. It's not going so well. You look like a wookie struck by lightning. You take a selfie but decide not to send it.

hee hee!

6. Sofia sneaks Ryan's phone out of his jacket and types a message to Abby: `Hi, Abby, I really like you! Ryan` "This is going to be good," Sofia says. But you wouldn't want anybody to do that to you. "No, Sofia," you say. "Don't send that."

7. Taylor has been kicked out of the game all week by an avatar named Tricky Tiger. You know Amelia is Tricky Tiger. You say, "Amelia, what's the deal with excluding Taylor? Stop it. She feels awful. You should tell her it's you and apologize."

8. You want to break up with Zach. It's WAY too awkward to do it in person, so you just post a notice online.

9. The posts on the discussion board are piling up. Wow. It's mean, mean stuff about Evelyn. Can what they say be true? You don't write anything, but you keep reading.

Answers

1. **Don't expect privacy online.** When you send something, it's out of your control. 100 percent.

2. **Don't share passwords.** The only people who should know your passwords are your parents. They own the accounts. Chances are, they own the devices. Their access protects you in all kinds of ways.

But sharing passwords with friends? No. Passwords aren't like a piece of jewelry that you trade to show your affection. They give people access to your whole private world: messages with your parents, messages with other friends. You aren't just violating your own privacy. You're violating the privacy of everybody who communicates with you.

Also, be practical. Friends get curious. Friends get mischievous. Friends get pressured into doing things. And friendships change. Protecting yourself online is often about setting smart limits on what you will and won't do. Keeping passwords to yourself is a big one.

3. **Don't forward messages.** When a friend sends a message just to you, it's been worded just for you. So respect your friend's privacy. Unless it's pure information ("Soccer practice was moved to 5:00"), don't pass a message on.

4. **Don't share embarrassing pictures of other people.** Friends can get silly with each other because they trust each other. That's why goofy photos exist. But share a goofy picture of a friend, and you're inviting the whole school to laugh at her.

5. **Don't share embarrassing pictures of yourself, either.** It's simple: If you'd be happy to see that photo of you posted on the front door at school, send it. If you wouldn't, don't.

6. **Don't pretend to be someone else.** Sending messages from someone else's device may seem like a harmless prank in the moment—and sometimes it probably *is* harmless, if everybody knows what has happened right away. But it's a joke designed to embarrass some-one, it hurts trust, and it's a very small step away from trickery that does real damage.

7. **Don't exclude people.** Excluding people online is as hurtful as excluding them in person—maybe even more so, because a girl like Taylor doesn't know who her enemies are, why she's being blocked, or what she's done to deserve it. She has no way to defend herself.

8. **Don't fight or break up in public.** Embarrassing somebody in public is bad. Doing it because you want to spare yourself an awkward conversation is worse. This boy deserves better.

9. **Don't view mean stuff.** You know not to join in on mean chats, and that's good. But reading itself is a kind of participation. It rewards the kids who are posting. Without an audience, these kids wouldn't be doing what they're doing. Say: "This is just mean. Not cool. I'm out of here"—and log off.

scenes from a drama

Reply!

Bella's text says: "jsyk dylan left. oh brooke telling him abt yestrdy. jen was there 2. :(imho u need to tell jake." Your heart flips over. Dylan? Brooke? Jen? Jake? Yesterday? Bella? What's happened? You're furious and scared. You don't know what to say, but you hit reply.

When you're anxious or mad, every cell in your body may want to fire off a reply that very instant. Don't do it. Walk away from the screen. Set the alarm for an hour and don't go back till it rings. Take a shower. Talk to your mom. Run around the block. Shoot baskets. The extra time gives you a chance to calm down and think: *How should I respond? What might happen if I said this as opposed to that?* If there's a lot at stake, write the message, save it, and reread it in an hour. An enormous amount of drama happens because people react too fast. Slow it down.

Please, like me!

There's a cool website where you can put up a picture of yourself and other people can comment. Your friend did it, and one guy said she looked pretty. You take 20 selfies, pick the best one, upload it, and then hold your breath, thinking, *Please, like me!*

There are ways girls open themselves up for incredible hurt online, and this is one of them. People usually aren't on these sites to be nice or constructive—or even honest, for that matter. They are there to laugh and gasp—to make the best wisecracks, to enjoy outrageous conversations they couldn't have in the real world. Whatever form that takes under your photo, it's probably not going to make you feel good. You may come away liking yourself less, and that would be too bad.

Anonymous?

Everyone at the sleepover agrees: Lauren is a total stalker and the most annoying girl at school. You spend the night posting anonymous things about her and laughing yourselves silly. In the morning, you think, *Whew. Glad no one knows who we are.*

People may not know who you are now, but they can find out. Every website can trace a post to a member if it wants to. If Lauren or her parents complained, they could identify you all, get your accounts blocked, and depending on what else has been going on, report you to the school as cyberbullies. Will that happen? Who knows. But forget anonymous. There are no secrets at a slumber party. Word will get out regardless. People will talk. Chances are, Lauren will know who was involved before you have to look her in the eye in science class.

Very clever

You're very clever, you're very funny, and you love writing about the silly things people do. Everyone reads your Top Ten posts, and your "worst hair" poll is legendary. If certain people have a problem with you—well, they shouldn't be so sensitive.

Humor has a glorious history. Getting people to laugh at themselves, poking fun at pretentions—it's what the best comics do. BUT. You're not on TV, making jokes about rich and powerful people. You're in a small community called a school, writing about kids who worry all the time about being liked and accepted, and whose worst nightmare is having other kids laugh at them. So do something else with all that creative energy. Write a book or a play instead. You can make up all the characters you want, have every bit as much fun, and share your wit with every kid in the school without hurting any of them.

secrets

Sharing a secret with another girl is a way of saying, *I trust you. You're special to me. We're close.* If you're excited or troubled, it feels good to have someone to confide in. But put other friends into the mix and things can change pretty fast. Does this sound familiar?

I like Chris. But don't tell!

I won't!

You know a secret. That secret feels like a little gold coin in your pocket. You're special. You've got something valuable. The problem is that nobody knows you have it.

I know who Silvana likes.

Really?

So maybe you drop a teeny-tiny hint. You want people to know that you know more than they do. You want them to know how close you are to your friend.

Now you're the center of attention. You refuse to tell. But once others know that the secret exists, they'll want to pry it out of you and will be ticked off if you clam up.

I can't tell.

I won't tell anyone!

I promised!

Is it Chris?

You want to tell. Your brain starts to whir: Maybe that coin in your pocket could buy you something here. If you tell, maybe this other girl will like you more. What's the harm, after all? She won't tell anybody. She promised. And, anyway, most people probably know already. Your friend shouldn't be so hush-hush about it.

The moment arrives.
There are two ways this can end.

1. You tell.

You give this other girl that little coin in your pocket. Is she a better friend now? No. Are you closer to her? No. You can't buy friends by betraying other friends. You haven't gained anything. But she has. She's got something she can use to hurt both your friend and your friendship. What will she do with it? Who knows. Whatever she likes. It's all in her hands.

How do you feel at this moment? Not happy. You're too busy dreading the moment your friend finds out what you've done.

How will she feel about you? Not good.

And what can you expect from other people when *you* need a friend to confide in? Not much.

Yes. It's Chris.

I knew it!

2. You don't tell.

You may get some blowback from people who wish you would talk, but it will pass.

When the dust clears, you walk off as a girl someone can trust. You didn't do the easy thing. You didn't do the tempting thing. You did the right thing. You'll like yourself for that, and other people will like you more, too. You can look forward to deeper friendships, and you still have that bright little coin of trust in your pocket.

Sorry. I shouldn't have brought it up.

Humph. Well, OK.

That's how it works.
You get to choose.

rewrite the script

People may think drama is inevitable. It isn't.
Girls like you can rewrite the script.

All girls gossip.
We can't live without it.

Nobody has any control
over what people do online,
so why fight it?

We share everything.
Everybody does.

Technology lets us
communicate better.
It helps build great
friendships.

I won't use gossip and rumors as weapons against other kids—in person or online.

I think before I send. I ask myself: *Is it clear? Is it fair? How will the other person feel about this? Will I be sorry I sent it?*

I'm not going to trade in secrets. My friends can trust me.

I don't overshare with friends. I keep some things private. It protects me.

My devices let me learn, work, listen, watch, see, and share. They're fun! But they don't run my life. I can turn them off and walk away.

Technology isn't for fights. If I have a problem with somebody, we'll talk it out in person.

out of control

75

training your brain

Which answer sounds most like you?

1. Julissa never talks and seems to have no friends. Now the teacher makes you study partners. Your first reaction is: *Oh, not Julissa!* Then you . . .

a. remind yourself that you've never even talked to Julissa. Who knows what her story is? It could be interesting to find out.

b. ask the teacher to give you someone else.

2. The new boy in the next desk has messy hair and a worn hoodie with a teddy bear on it. Your first reaction is: *That kid is seriously weird!* Then you . . .

a. remind yourself that weird can be good. You smile at him.

b. turn away. You don't want to get connected to someone like that.

3. Magda quit talking to you the day she started sitting with Soo Jin. That was last year. Now Soo Jin is sitting with the popular kids, and Magda is sitting alone. Your first reaction is: *Serves her right.* Then you . . .

a. remember how horrible you felt when you got dumped, and invite Magda to sit with you.

b. turn your back. You hope Magda's alone the whole year.

4. Once again, Jazmin is making fun of Amelia. Your first reaction is: *I don't like what Jazmin's doing, but I don't want to make a big drama about it.* Then you . . .

   a. think about how horrible Amelia must feel and tell Jazmin to lay off.

   b. shrug. Amelia is used to it.

5. Nathan walks straight to the front as if there weren't a line. As always. Your first reaction is: *He's the rudest, meanest kid in the entire school.* Then you . . .

   a. try to imagine why a person could act like that and decide he must feel really bad inside. What might he be like if he weren't so angry all the time?

   b. decide he's a horrible person.

Answers

If you checked mostly a's, you've trained your brain to connect with people. You may have plenty of judgmental thoughts (we all do), but you don't go with them. When they come up, you stop. You notice what's happening. You wonder: *What would it be like to be that other person?* That gives you empathy. It means you lean toward acceptance. You lean toward understanding. It makes you more open and less fearful.

If you checked mostly b's, you tend to go with your first, gut reactions. If those are negative, you don't question them. You end up judging people harshly, almost without realizing you're doing it. So start noticing the dialogue going on inside your head. Ask yourself: *What am I feeling? What words are shaping my thoughts?* If they're unkind, find more generous ones. You're not covering up how you feel—you're training yourself to be more compassionate. You're training your brain to admit what you know in your deepest self to be true: that you're not so different from these other kids, and they're not so different from you.

getting ugly

Here are some common reasons kids use for doing mean things to one another. Let's count the good ones.

There are the reasons people say out loud.

"She deserves it. She did something bad."

"She hurt my feelings."

"She betrayed me."

"I have a right to get her back."

"We're in a fight. How else CAN we behave?"

There are the reasons people *don't* say out loud.

"She's stuck-up. She needs to be put in her place."

"She competes with me. She's my enemy."

"I have to do what my friends are doing."

"She scares me. She's so different."

"I want to be sure nobody thinks I'm like HER."

"I'm so unhappy. I want to make somebody else unhappy, too."

"It's fun."

"Being a little mean makes me more popular. Nobody messes with me!"

There are justifications.

"We just got a little carried away."

"She can give as good as she gets."

"I agree people should be nice.
But this is different.
You don't understand."

There are the ways people pretend nothing is going on at all.

"It's not THAT mean."

"She's too sensitive."

"She can't take a joke."

"We're just playing around."

How many good reasons are there?

Zero.

There is no right way to be unkind to somebody else. So if you see kids trying to excuse themselves for being mean, tell them not to bother. There's nothing that turns that tar into gold.

Cruelty is wrong. Story over.

when you're bullied

When you're bullied, life can be a waking nightmare.

You may feel ashamed.

What's wrong with me?

What have I done?

You may feel desperate.

How can I change?

What can I do to make them like me?

What can I do to make them stop?

At first, you may wonder why no one will help you.

After days and months, you may think no one *can* help you.

Worst of all, you may get so used to the abuse that you come to think you deserve it. You don't. You don't deserve one bit of it. Tell yourself that loud and clear. Say it as you board the bus. Say it in the halls. Say it as you go to sleep at night.

I don't deserve this.

Then steel your mind to go to work on this difficult problem. There are no quick fixes, but there is hope, and it starts here: Don't cooperate with your bully by acting the way she expects you to. You'll find out you're stronger than you think.

A bully wants you to lose control.

A kid who bullies wants you to cry or lose your temper. It shows she's getting to you. Don't take the bait.

Don't start a physical fight. (You could end up hurt or suspended from school.) Don't try to taunt back. (A bully's probably better at it than you are.) Don't beg or plead for the bullies to stop. (Bullies love that.) Don't pretend the abuse isn't happening, either. (It obviously is.)

Instead, take charge by pulling the plug on the situation. You don't have to be clever or make a big speech. You just need to end it: "I don't need to listen to this. I'm out of here." "This is just stupid. I'm leaving." "Thanks, but no thanks." If you can't move away, put in the earbuds and turn up the music.

You should do the same kind of thing if the bullying is online. Kids who bully want their victims to respond to insulting posts so they can keep the nasty stuff going. Get off the site and block the sender. Give the bully a big blank wall to work with.

A bully wants to intimidate you.

You may be scared—and that's OK. There are times it makes sense to be. But don't let your body show it. Make a conscious effort to stand up straight. Look people in the eye. It's not easy to do when you're terrified inside, but try anyway—and keep trying. Standing tall doesn't just make you look more confident. It helps you feel that way, too.

There may also be times (when a bully isn't surrounded by her friends) that you can surprise her by speaking up for yourself:

Bully: "Hey there, Ugly."

You: "You call me terrible names all the time. I want you to stop. I have a right to come to school without you and your friends saying cruel things about me."

Bully: "And you're going to make me?"

You: "I'm saying you're wrong to treat me like this. You should stop. I've said what I had to say. Now I'm done."

Is this going to make the bully apologize and change her ways? Not likely. But it will change you. You will have looked that girl in the eye and told her what she should do. That makes you stronger. **81**

A bully wants you isolated.

Kids who bully want you to be alone. They don't want you surrounded by friends who'll defend you—and they definitely don't want adults to know what they're doing. They need your silence.

Don't give it to them. Tell your parents. Tell a teacher or a counselor. Tell an adult you trust. Open the windows and let the light shine in on this ugly game. A bully will call it "tattling" (naturally). In fact, it's you being strong and resourceful. You're getting the help you need.

Once you have some allies, you can come up with a plan together. It might go something like this:

1. Write down everything that Abby did last week.

2. Copy her messages from the computer and my phone.

3. Go with Mom and Dad to talk to Mr. Toshibi, the principal. We'll tell him what Abby's been doing and show him the evidence.

4. We'll ask if I can have early lunch so I can eat with my friends Sarah and Til, and we'll brainstorm other ways I can have my friends around to help protect me.

5. We'll ask Mr. Toshibi to talk to Abby's parents.

6. I won't walk down hallway B after school. I won't let Abby and her friends get me alone.

7. Mom will e-mail that one website about the posts.

8. Dad will call the cell-phone company.

9. I'll start doing gymnastics twice a week. I'll do other things suggested on pages 48–49 of my Drama book so that I've got something fun to think about.

10. My neighbor Micah is always nice to me. Maybe she or her 10th-grade friends have ideas that can help.

11. If . . .

Make a detailed record.

As part of any plan, you'll need to make a record of what's been going on, to help explain it to others. Write down the dates, times, and locations of important incidents. Document your digital world, too, with screenshots and printouts of bad posts, messages, and e-mails. A social-media website can use those things to help identify anonymous senders. Your parents can also talk to your Internet and cell-phone providers about removing posts and revoking the bully's account.

Getting adults involved may make you nervous. You may feel like you're losing control of what happens next. It's really the opposite. You're taking control back from the bully. You're refusing to play the rotten role she's written for you.

A bully wants you to think this is about you.

It's not. It's about the bully. Kids who bully are usually more powerful at school than their targets, and they enjoy that. But they aren't strong or confident inside. If they were, they wouldn't need to hurt others to make themselves feel stronger. Remember that if you're ever tempted to think *Why me?* and start hating yourself. There is nothing in you that needs fixing. There is nothing in you to repair. You are fine exactly the way you are. The bully is the one with the problem, and the bully is the one who should change.

It will get better.

The bullying will stop eventually. Believe it: *It's going to get better.* Your task from here to there is to believe in yourself. And when you look back on this time of your life, you will see a girl you can be proud of.

looking on

Kids who bully are surrounded by kids who don't like what they're doing. So why doesn't anybody stop the bullying? Bystanders can give you plenty of reasons.

My friends are doing it. I have to go along.

If I speak up, they'll turn on me.

If I speak up, they'll just get worse.

It's not my business.

I don't want to rat on them. Everybody hates a tattletale.

I have no idea what to do to stop this.

I don't like this, but nobody else is doing anything!

But the biggest reason is that the community—the school and the kids in it—tolerates meanness. It's expected. It's accepted. When something ugly happens, kids don't say, "Hey, we don't do that here." It's more like, "Yeah, we've seen that. It happens."

True, you may be thinking, *but a single girl is never going to change THAT.* Maybe yes, maybe no. But you don't need to be the hero of the Western world. You can start with the small stuff.

Don't play along with a bully.

You can send the message that you don't like what's happening. Don't laugh at the ugly joke. Don't participate in the mean conversation. Don't forward the text. Don't repeat the rumor. Pick up your books and walk off.

You're not confronting the bully directly, but this kind of resistance makes a difference. Kids look to other kids for cues. They'll think: *If she can opt out, maybe I can—and maybe I should.*

Sympathize.

You can also go up to the bullied kid later and say, "Are you OK? That was bad. I'm sorry." Your sympathy tells her she's not crazy—she really was verbally attacked, even though no one reacted. It also tells her that you know it was wrong. That can mean the world.

Speak up.

The time may come when you feel able to speak out. Do it! You can say something short and neutral:

"Chill out."   "Ease up."   "That's enough."

You can say something stronger:

"Why are you doing this?"   "Stop it."   "This isn't right."

Are there risks? Yes. You need to think about what's safe and what's realistic. But when bystanders speak up, it matters. It cracks the shell of acceptance. Kids who bully want an audience and an easy victim. If they know public opinion is moving against them, it changes a lot.

Report it.

If someone is being physically threatened, or if the abuse is vicious or prolonged, you have to tell an adult. You have no choice. If the bully calls you a tattletale, you can fairly answer: "Get real. I'm getting somebody OUT of trouble. If you're IN trouble, it's your own fault."

Make it the new normal.

Make a decision: You're going to be a kid who resists bullying. You're learning how, and you'll keep learning. You'll soon discover that many other kids feel the way you do. Together you can make a new normal. You don't start from, *Yeah, that happens.* You start from, *That is totally uncool and unacceptable.* Together, you begin to change your school.

Along the way, you will be giving hope and respect to people who profoundly need it. To them, you actually *are* the hero of the Western world.

forgiveness

Two years ago, this one girl bullied me horribly. Now she's nice to me. All my friends expect me to forgive her because "she's changed—she's so sweet now." But I can't. The memory haunts me. I can still see her sneer when she said that no one liked me and I should give up on life. I don't think I'll ever be able to forgive her or get over it. Is that wrong?—Bullied

No, it's not wrong. You feel how you feel. You can't fake that away. And despite what your friends say, you don't owe this girl forgiveness or anything else. That said, something needs to change. The bullying is alive inside you when you're with your friends at school. You're still struggling with fear, shame, and anger. You deserve to be happier than this, and you can be.

Make it a goal: *I want to feel better.* Then start changing the channel when these dark memories come up. Instead of reliving a horrible moment, turn your mind to one that gave you joy. If your brain flips back to the bad stuff (it probably will), just take some slow, deep breaths and turn it around again. Tell yourself you're breaking a habit. Expressing your feelings can help, too. Write or paint them out. Talk to an older person, ideally a counselor.

Also, if you've never talked openly with the girl who haunts you, now might be the time. The point is not to attack her. The point is to talk about what happened. Ask: "Do you ever think about fifth grade? I do." She may be defensive, but she also might be ready to talk. What was going through her mind back then? Does she understand what it meant to you? Having some answers may help you, and having had the strength to bring this out of the shadows can help as well. Healing is a process of many steps, big and small. This can be one of them.

Everyone says that I'm so nice and so pretty and so caring, but when I look in the mirror I see an ugly, mean girl struggling with anger. I have been a jerk and a queen bee, and I completely hate myself. How can I turn around and be the nice, loving girl I was before?—Mean Girl

You don't need to go back to third grade. You just need to go back to being yourself.

Apologizing is a good place to start. Who got hurt when you were being "a jerk"? Go to them and say you're sorry: "I've been thinking about how I behaved last year. I teased you all the time. It was mean. I know I hurt you, and I'm really sorry." Do what you can to repair the damage. If you told a lie, correct it. If you destroyed a friendship, go to the people involved and explain what you did.

The goal here is not forgiveness. Your victim might forgive you or she might not—that will be her choice. The goal is to make this other girl's life better. Chances are, she's been struggling with pain and anger every bit as much as you are. You want to free her from that.

Yet apologizing can help you, too. It helps because you are throwing off the fake "you" and doing something you know is right. You've stopped pretending to be perfectly pretty and nice. You've started being real.

You can like yourself for that, and maybe start forgiving yourself, too. You may have bullied somebody. That doesn't make you a bully for life. You have plenty of time to take what you've learned and become the person you want to be. It all starts with what you do next.

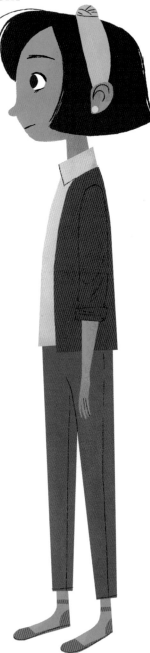

rewrite
the script

What if no one ever teased anyone
about hair or clothes or family
or anything else? What if we
all thought about the impact of
what we said before saying it?
Then maybe the only place drama
would exist is on the stage.
—Cierra

casting call

Quiet backstage! The lights are going down. The curtain is rising. The show's about to begin. This time don't pick the part you *might* play. Pick the part you *want* to play.

Scene 1

The drama between Zoey and Trinity has been going three days straight.

a. You talk, text, talk, text, get angry, get sad, get confused, chat online, and lose sleep. Needless to say, your big presentation does not go well.

b. You tell Zoey and Trinity that they should talk with each other directly and figure it out.

Scene 2

Yesterday you told Jaycee your secret. Now she's told it to Taylor.

a. You act like it's nothing, but inside you're thinking, *Just you wait, Jaycee. I'll get you back.* You know things about her, you know how to use them, and you will.

b. You find Jaycee and say, "I asked you not to tell anybody. You broke your promise. I'm mad. If you want to be friends, you can't do that to me again."

Scene 3

You're brooding about Ashley when your little sister throws herself on your bed. Notebooks go flying. Argh!

a. You yell at your sister and get grounded. Stuff like this happens to you *all . . . the . . . time.* Life is unfair.

b. You stop and ask yourself, *Why am I so mad?* Talking through your feelings calms you down and helps you identify the real problem: Ashley. So after your sis helps pick up your stuff, you call your friend and say, "Can we talk?"

Scene 4

Sophia has decided she doesn't like Amber. Now she says you and your other friends should stop liking Amber, too.

a. What Sophia says goes. If she tells you to stop talking to Amber, you'll do it. If she wants to exclude Amber, OK. If she thinks you should make jokes about Amber, or whisper and spread stories about her— that's what you'll have to do. You're sorry for Amber, but there's no bucking Sophia.

b. You tell Sophia no. She can't order you around. She shouldn't be ordering other people around either, and—by the way—it's wrong to mess with other people's relationships.

Scene 5

You're with your friends.

a. You feel fake.

b. You feel great!

Answer

Did you pick lots of a's? Didn't think so. Why would you? You want to be happy. You don't want drama to eat up your life. You don't want drama in one part of your life to feed drama in another, either. You want to be able to speak freely with your friends about how you feel. You want to speak up for what you deserve and to disagree when you have to. You want friendships based on affection—not on power, rules, and exclusion. And guess what? You can have them! You're ready to turn the page on drama and play the best role in the world: being you.

a world without drama

What would a world without drama look like?

Anna, Emma, and Gracie signed up for the talent show together. They disagree about the song, but they'll figure it out.

Jason broke up with Bianca. She was sad, but Jasmine cheered her up.

Ava, Aaliyah, and Lila are volunteering once a week at a nursing home. Ava's mom drives them.

There's a new girl in school. She always wears purple. She taught Min-joo how to use a pottery wheel.

Katie's big clarinet solo is tonight. Maya sent her a text that said: "Go get 'em, KT. You rock! ♥"

Olivia's got Liam doing yoga.

Rachel started a school newspaper. Mikayla's doing cartoons for it.

Nice!

Life without drama is better. Kids will always have problems. That's just part of being human. People will always make mistakes and do things they shouldn't do. But it's all ten times easier to handle without the drama. You can see what's really going on. Conflicts don't blow up into full-force hurricanes. Relationships are more relaxed, less fearful.

If your own school is Drama Central, this possibility may seem to be a long way off. But if you cool down the drama in your own life, your friends have a chance to rethink drama, too. You can build on that.

Try talking to your close friends about drama. Use this book, if it helps. Take the quizzes together. Talk about similar issues in your own friendships. Read the **rewrite the script** pages and have a debate: What lines ring true? What lines don't? Are there ways to put some of those ideas to work in your own lives? How can you help one another do that?

Make a pact for how you'll treat one another, too. You won't always live up to your ideals, but if you keep trying, you'll get better at it. Little by little, you'll be more open and honest. You will trust one another more. You'll give one another the strength and courage to be yourselves. And when you walk in the door at school, you'll bring all that with you. You may be surprised just how far those ripples can spread.

It can start with you. It can start now.

Do you have true tales of drama to share?
Have you found ways to lower it in your life,
shrink it at your school,
or free your friends from it?
Please let us know what happened
and what you did!

Write to
***Drama, Rumors & Secrets* Editor**
American Girl
8400 Fairway Place
Middleton, WI 53562

Here are some other American Girl books you might like:

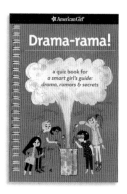

Discover online games, quizzes, activities,
and more at americangirl.com